CONTEN

C000184745

Poetry Book Society

CHOICE RECOMMENDATION SPECIAL COMMENDATION SELECTORS	VONA GROARKE & TIM LIARDET
TRANSLATION SELECTOR	GEORGE SZIRTES
PAMPHLET SELECTORS	A. B. JACKSON DENISE SAUL
GUEST SELECTOR	ANDREW McMILLAN
CONTRIBUTORS	ALICE KATE MULLEN NATHANIEL SPAIN INPRESS TEAM
EDITORIAL & DESIGN	ALICE KATE MULLEN

Membership Options

Associate - *4 bulletins a year* (UK £18, Europe £20, Overseas £23)
Full - *4 books and 4 bulletins a year* (£55, £65, £75)
Charter - *20 books and 4 bulletins* (£170, £185, £215)
Education - *4 books, 4 bulletins and teaching notes* (£58, £68, £78)
Charter Education - *20 books, 4 bulletins and teaching notes* (£180, £195, £225)
Translation - *4 Recommended translations and 4 bulletins* (£70, £100, £118)
Student - *4 books and 4 bulletins* (£27, £47, £57)
Single copies £5

Subscribe at www.poetrybooks.co.uk
Cover artwork by Nancy Campbell http://nancycampbell.co.uk/
Copyright Poetry Book Society and contributors. All rights reserved.
ISBN 978-1-9998589-0-2   ISSN 0551-1690

Supported using public funding by
ARTS COUNCIL ENGLAND

Poetry Book Society | Inpress Books | Churchill House | 12 Mosley Street |
Newcastle upon Tyne | NE1 1DE | 0191 230 8100 | pbs@inpressbooks.co.uk

LETTER FROM THE PBS

I would like to start with a huge thank you to our poet selector, Vona Groarke, who has come to the end of her PBS tenure with this Winter *Bulletin*. Vona has made some brilliant selections and written wonderful reviews over the last two years and has been incredibly supportive to myself and the team since we took over the running of the PBS for which I am eternally grateful. We wish her well and look forward to reviewing her future titles!

We are delighted to welcome Sandeep Parmar as our new Book Selector, Sandeep is the author of two poetry collections and is a Ledbury Forte prize winner. She was a Forward Prize 2017 judge and has written for a wide variety of publications, including the *Guardian*, *TLS*, *FT* and *Poetry Review*.

You may have noticed some changes, not only in the design of the *Bulletin*, but also a new guest selector spot – Andrew McMillan has chosen his favourite title of 2017 for this *Bulletin*, watch this space for further guest selections. Jen Campbell, award winning poet, reviewer and vlogger (video blogger for the uninitiated!) will be reviewing PBS selections on Youtube – we can't wait to view her reviews of the Winter selected titles in early December.

Please do keep an eye on our events pages too, we are really keen to showcase the PBS selected poets and relish the opportunity to meet our members face to face. On that note, we will be launching this *Bulletin* at the Poetry Café in London on the 8th December and we would love to see as many of you as possible there. For those of you who are students – we are relaunching the PBS Student Poetry Prize later in October. Visit our website for further details soon.

Finally, the selections. Sasha Dugdale is this season's Choice with the fantastic *Joy*, the award winning title poem has been described as a "masterly accomplishment". We have a wonderful mix of Recommendations with collections from Paul Deaton, Tim Dooley, Anne Michaels and Ahren Warner. Fleur Adcock receives the Special Commendation with *Hoard* and Recommended Translation goes to the translation of Romanian poet Ana Blandiana by Paul Scott Derrick and Viorica Patea. Pamphlet Choice is awarded to the "tender, hard and amused poems" that make up *Guppy Primer* from Ruth McIlroy.

- Sophie O'Neill, PBS and Inpress Director

4

SASHA DUGDALE

Sasha Dugdale is a poet, translator and editor. She has published four collections of poetry, the most recent of which is *Joy* (Carcanet, 2017). Her long poem 'Joy' won the Forward Prize for Best Single Poem in 2016. In 2017 she won a Cholmondeley Award. She is currently working on translations of Maria Stepanova's poems for publication in the UK. Sasha was editor of *Modern Poetry in Translation* for five years, and co-editor of the international anthology *Centres of Cataclysm* (Bloodaxe, 2016).

JOY

CARCANET | £9.99 | PBS PRICE £7.50

Sasha Dugdale's *Joy*, her fourth collection, is unquestionably her most explorative book so far, dominated by the thirteen-page title poem with which it opens. Moving in its moods and tonal variations the poem is a masterly accomplishment. Catherine Blake, William's recent widow, remembers how they met "...a thousand years ago" and speaks her way, groove by groove, through the complex cycles of her grief. Presented almost as a one-act play, the monologue shifts between lament and contemplation, anger and sorrowing, hope and remorse, the anguish caused by the impossible absence and the presence of that absence:

I am a rent shirt... I am a poor man's shirt and a pair of woollen stockings and a patched jacket thrown from the hearse... Every breeze shudders me... And no one wants me...

How I ache.... How I ache... How I ache...

This book is comprised of only sixteen poems which testify to Dugdale's powers of focus on the one hand, and her development of the long, and longer, poem on the other. After the deeply excavatory title poem, which often inhabits the clay-rich soils located somewhere between poetry and prose, Dugdale takes leave to put on display her tight, formal virtuosity in the shape of rhyming quatrains, couplets and a villanelle. The five pages of 'The Canoe,' and the erudite sequencing over six pages of 'Days' – based upon the war experiences of Svetlana Alexievich – are in many ways as impressive as the title poem.

Dugdale is very good indeed at spinning narratives while supplying them with rationale and purpose without the crunch line or exaggerate finale. She never belabours meaning. "War is liquid-thought-fire," she writes in 'Days', as the storyline tilts the text towards revelation made clear by its precise and effulgent telling.

| SELECTORS' COMMENT

TIM LIARDET

SASHA DUGDALE

My collection *Joy* takes its name from a long poem which is a substantial part of the collection. The poem 'Joy' is a dramatic monologue, spoken by Catherine Blake, the wife and helpmate of poet, artist and visionary William Blake. Catherine, or Kate, is speaking after Blake's death in 1827 and her speech is a consideration of her life as the partner of a creative genius, as well as an examination of her own role in Blake's creativity. In order to write the poem I spent months studying Blake's work and his drawings. At first I wasn't sure how to write about Blake because he was an enigma to me in many ways: his work seeming to spring out of nowhere, his visions wonderful but disconcerting. However I found myself more and more intrigued by the relationship between him and Catherine, his closest friend, colleague and co-creator. Catherine's voice is barely recorded, so it didn't feel impertinent to imagine her grief after his death, or even her reflections about the long life they had lived together.

This collection includes two other longer sequences: 'The Canoe' which is a very deliberate meditation on history and our relationship with history and myth. It was inspired by a long canoe from Oceania I saw in the Musée du quai Branly in Paris. The other longer poem is called 'Days' and it was a response to Svetlana Alexievich's book about women in wartime which I read in Russian, but which has recently been translated as *The Unwomanly Face of War*. Both of these poems seem to have gained a horrid relevance since I wrote them a couple of years ago and that disturbs me. A number of intellectual themes that have consciously bothered me for years have found lyrical expression in poems in this collection and that pleases me, because it is increasingly hard to write poetry "in these bad times".

SASHA RECOMMENDS

My list of must-reads would include Kim Hyesoon, the powerful Korean poet (*I'm OK, I'm Pig!* is published by Bloodaxe), and her equally compelling poet-translator Don Mee Choi (*Hardly War* is published by Wave Books in the USA). Adnan Al-Sayegh, the Iraqi poet who is published by Arc in Stephen Watts' translation, (*Pages From The Biography of an Exile*) and Stephen also translates a fine Syrian poet Golan Haji whose work has just been published in English translation: *A Tree Whose Name I Don't Know* (A Midsummer Night's Press).

I CHOICE

VILLANELLE

When an ordinary man dies
Like that, all of a sudden,
There is no darkening of the skies,

Outside the lawns remain green and sodden
And vegetables pulled for supper lie
There is no sudden darkening of the sky

You can see the path his boots have trodden
The boots that slowly fold and subside
When an ordinary man dies

How ordinary! The cats still need feeding
The unbidden sun must endlessly rise
There is no sudden darkening of the skies

The shed is oven warm and full of flies
The beds grow and want weeding
When an ordinary man dies

It is a thing of great surprise
That no curtain is rent, no sacrifice lies bleeding
There is no sudden darkening of the skies

Only the ordinary parting with other lives –
The barely audible tearing of ties
And no sudden darkening of the skies
When an ordinary man dies.

KITTIWAKE

Your jizz, little gull, is the traveller's
jizz, the wanderer, who sees the black, flecked ocean
barren like the steppe, and drops to feel the cut of its
rough coat, sail boat-like in the dizzying swell
and lift again, casual as the inhabitant of a planet poisonous to man.
No doubt you might have hung around
but all the accommodation offered to you was the white tenement
blasted with guano, crumbling with the chalk's sickness
the clamour of children from the playground in the yard.
Those wings, tipped with ink, as if you had signed the dotted line
With one, signed up to country and nation and place –
            then in an instant turned mid-air
                    and dipped the other wing in the bottle
to run your signature through. Not citizen! Not patriot! Not I –
from now on the expanse and the blackness will be my place,
amongst you I will make no home, only a perch
as fishermen perched on the edge of a hostile continent,
so the kittiwake will perch, briefly, all the better to fear
You – the inland, the citizen.

Image credit John Sen

PAUL DEATON

Paul Deaton was born in London and raised in Wales. His poems appear regularly in *The Spectator* and are included in York Notes for GCSE study guides. He lives in Bristol and works as a freelance editor of art books, for the NHS and as an addictions counsellor. He reads regularly with his Bristol workshop group The Spoke.

A WATCHFUL ASTRONOMY

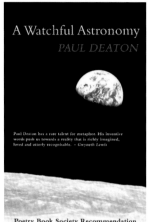

A Watchful Astronomy
PAUL DEATON

Paul Deaton has a rare talent for metaphor. His inventive words push us towards a reality that is richly imagined, loved and utterly recognisable. – *Gwyneth Lewis*

Poetry Book Society Recommendation

SEREN | £9.99 | PBS PRICE £7.50

I hold the space between stars,
The hour's no-hour.
And, as in alleyways, I hold too, the concentrated
                                            blackness.
- That Bang

There's a strong play with perspective in these poems, contrasting the close-up with the panoramic and pitting intimacy against the sometimes unfathomable distances between people. In Part 1, the dominant presence is a father who looms large and inscrutable, physically dominant if emotionally taciturn. The poems ply the gaps between what is asked of him and what is received: if they are tenderly disappointed in the way the relationship buckles or falters, they look to the natural world for context and recourse, finding there a vocabulary and imagery to gather in the sense of bewilderment and by contrast, the strange consolations of landscape and place. There's an appealing richness to these descriptions, as in 'Year's End':

> The year backs into darkness.
> The hills hold a vow of silence.
> Stood above the Tinkertoy farms
> has it always been like this?

The parental relationship, in comparison, is treated in starker language that is pared back to fact and narrative, as if to enact a determined terseness and lack of colour. It seems this relationship is perennially winter-struck, all growth suspended and promise stunted. There's little doubt as to where the poems' strongest attentions are directed. If occasionally, those poems that feature particular characters trim the tone and register so close to the bone that little in the way of movement or energy is possible, this is countered with poems nicely alert to descriptive detail, that open out generously and confidently, as in the final two stanzas of 'Late Hour':

> ...Our world
> shrinks to the white width of the bedroom's lens.
>
> Night thickens and the wall
> listens. A desert sphinx, a blank Buddha,
> it says nothing, a nothing, that is all.

PAUL DEATON

I read recently "many people feel themselves to be searching repeatedly for the contact they missed as children" (Susie Orbach). I think there is an aspect of that going on here. When your trust with humans has been a struggle you need somewhere else, something else to transpose yourself onto. I'm looking for contact in my poems, with my past, parents and partner but also with nature and the wider universe; something primary, which quite possibly is an echo of the aloneness I felt in childhood.

I've come to realise, slowly, that this aloneness is part of life's paradox and in Winnicottian terms, is not and should not be resolved, but it is made knowable and bearable through the transitional object of writing poems. I say bear(able), but this seeking oftentimes feels a magical act.

In this book I have a sense of reclaiming myself out of stuckness and self-denial. That it is ok. That I have the power to be. Reading Kay Redfield Jamison's memoir *An Unquiet Mind* a number of years ago was a turning point. I realised through that book that I was enough. What I needed to do was commit. I'd been writing for years but for years it was a closet hobby. A guilty pleasure. I didn't share it or own it.

Knowing who we are is not an easy journey. A lot of my life I have not wanted to, but the push to know has strangely won out. These few poems are my journey into life. To know who I am. My attempt to make life meaningful. Without meaning, which isn't given, but created, there is no life at all. Meaning or death. Poems or death. I'm not aiming at anything grand: just trying to work out the narrative of my life in the complexity of living it.

PAUL RECOMMENDS

Boris Pasternak's poems have always been my touchstone.

RECOMMENDATION

14

...Our world
shrinks to the white width of the bedroom's lens.

SEA BREAM DINNER

And sometimes it is enough to only
think about what to have for dinner,
and to go out to the shops in advance
through the square beneath the lurching
horse chestnuts, and over the long broken
path slabs at midday, to buy fish, fresh
from the fishmonger's magician
hands and to get home in the evening,
to cook with stained spoon and heavy pan
what has been found first by a Cornish fisherman.

And not to be in a devil's rush, not to high
hurdle against the odds a sprinter's dinner,
but to gas light the stove, to put
the whole sea bream in the clay tagine
carefully, as if it were your own parents
you were laying to rest, with sprig
of bay, splash of wine, slide this day's death
into the oven with a softly worded message,
be wholesome, silver sea thing,
treasured, let the white meat do its best.

TIM DOOLEY

Tim Dooley is a tutor for The Poetry School and a visiting lecturer at the University of Westminster. He was a teacher for many years and from 2008 to 2017 reviews editor of *Poetry London*. His first collection of poems, *The Interrupted Dream*, was published by Anvil in 1985, followed by the pamphlets *The Secret Ministry* (2001) and *Tenderness* (2004), both from Smith/Doorstop. *Tenderness* was a Poetry Book Society Pamphlet Choice and *Keeping Time* (Salt, 2008) was a Poetry Book Society Recommendation. His selected poems, *The Sound We Make Ourselves: Poems 1971-2016*, was published by Eyewear in December 2016.

WEEMOED

EYEWEAR PUBLISHING | £10.99 | PBS PRICE £8.25

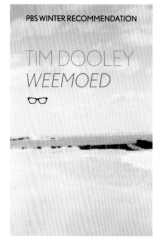

PBS WINTER RECOMMENDATION

TIM DOOLEY
WEEMOED

Vincent Van Gogh obligingly provides the explanation for the title word, but it's not given to us until page thirty-one, at the head of a sequence of twelve poems that dovetails the Dutch artist's description of drizzly Ramsgate dusk (where he was a short-order tutor at Mr. Stokes' boarding school), into a somewhat Larkinesque narrative recording of the suburban facts of a contemporary life refracted through the enquiring mind. Part three of the sequence reads, in its entirety:

'By the sadness of the countenance
the heart is made better'. He considers
the life of *un homme intérieur et
spirituel* as a possible career.

There are forces against this.
In the radio discussion
the possession of 'a wandering mind'
has just been described as 'a condition'.

In this urbane and stylish collection, diffidence is played against authority and wonder against ennui, so that when a Korean sculptor is mentioned (in 'Taking Down the Statue'), it is only a matter of four lines before the more monolithic presence of John Lewis is invoked. In 'Recent Events in Logres' (another of the seven sequences to which this collection commits), Arthurian legend shape-shifts into a contemporary register, and 'Politics' offers a bald rebuke to the Yeats poem of the same title:

There are small red hearts on your blouse
and your heart is on your sleeve
as you address the council chamber.

Sitting here on the balcony
my attention is fixed.

Sharp on politics, art, philosophy, *Weemoed* is at its savviest when it rounds on its summoned guardian poets (amongst them, Yeats, Heaney and Shakespeare), to strike the attitudes of *ars poetica*, as in the wry ending to the impressive 'Morning'.

SELECTORS' COMMENT

VONA GROARKE

TIM DOOLEY

One of the ways in which the writing in *Weemoed* differs from my earlier collections is that I have been able to tackle longer narratives and sequences, while retaining an interest in the short (sometimes very short) lyric. 'At the Coast', the first of the longer poems to be written, started as a technical experiment favouring the sentence over the line and developed into a meditation on the British seaside, in which it was perhaps inevitable that I would be drawn to images of childhood and family life.

Some of the shorter poems also follow personal experience: the death of parents, the birth of grandchildren, the early loss of friends and contemporaries. In other poems personal experience is refracted through outside sources. The title poem makes use of the Dutch word for melancholy, which Vincent Van Gogh argued could be read as a combination of sadness and courage. When I started reading Van Gogh's letters, the coincidence that he and I both spent time early in our lives as teachers in Ramsgate paved the way for a double narrative exploring the artist's use of experience.

There is doubling too in 'Recent Events in Logres', whose major source is the story of Merlin and Viviane in the French 'Vulgate Cycle' (a much more romantic version than that offered later by Malory). Retelling this story offered me the opportunity of writing a contemporary fable about the deliberate relinquishing of power. '12 x 12' by contrast is non-narrative, offering fleeting observations and snatches of experience while experimenting with the Korean sijo form.

The collection ends with two poems, a satire of protectionism and a eulogy to European endurance, prompted by the result of the 2016 referendum – a result at odds with the international vision (making connections across distance and time) that *Weemoed* seeks to celebrate.

TIM RECOMMENDS

Emily Berry, *Stranger Baby* (Faber)
Rachael Boast, *Void Studies* (Picador)
Kayo Chingonyi, *Kumukanda* (Chatto)
Jenna Clake, *Fortune Cookie* (Eyewear)
Luke Kennard, *Cain* (Penned in the Margins)
W. S. Merwin, *Garden Time* (Bloodaxe)
F. T. Prince, *Memoirs of Caravaggio / In Keats Country* (Perdika Editions)
Denise Riley, *Say Something Back* (Picador)

RECOMMENDATION

If one is patient, a half-light emerges and eventually the hard lines of your calling.

And that is the world you enter with your ice-scraper.

LOOSE LEAF

These old green or orange
paperbacks are falling
apart on us. Pages
dropping out, tobacco-
coloured, flaking at the
edges. Incipient
autumn is outside us
too: the bright yellow slips
of willow, or still green
oak-leaves curling as if
left too near the fire. The
low afternoon sun warm on
the back of the neck throws
light on the spire across
the road and the white rose
among the tight black curls
of the schoolgirl checking
her smartphone. In the park
there is time to admire
flashes of yellow and
red on the beak of this
coot-like bird and marvel
at the gloriousness
of now, unbothered
by the evening's chill.

Image credit Derek Shapton

ANNE MICHAELS

Anne Michaels is the author of the internationally bestselling novel *Fugitive Pieces*, which won multiple prizes including the Orange Prize and the *Guardian* Fiction Prize, and was made into a major film. Her second novel, *The Winter Vault*, was shortlisted for the Commonwealth Writers' Prize and longlisted for the International IMPAC Dublin Literary Award. She is also the author of several highly acclaimed poetry volumes, the selected volume *Poems*, and, most recently, *Correspondences*, which was shortlisted for the Griffin Poetry Prize. Her books have been translated into more than forty-five languages. Anne Michaels lives in Toronto, and is the city's Poet Laureate.

ALL WE SAW

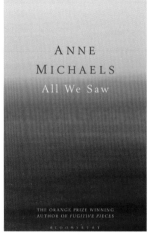

BLOOMSBURY | £16.99 | PBS PRICE £12.75

The poems of this collection are more than usually respectful of the white space surrounding them. In Parts I and IV, rarely does a page boast more than thirteen lines of type; the other parts seem positively profligate in comparison, though still given to frugality, in their way. Occasionally lines are isolated for effect, so that what would be a run-on in most poems is islanded, staccato-like, onto single lines occupying a whole page: page fifty-seven, for example, reads (in its entirety): "in the cemetery I understood" and page fifty-eight, "we keep what belongs to us".

To what end such an arrangement? It could be that poems which fix their gaze so purposefully on their own resonance and impact use the space as a medium, as an electric current might be said to use water. These are poems that do not shy away from the asking of big questions. In 'Ask Aloud', for example, a rather determined romantic imperative plays itself out in pronouncements and questions to which one suspects the poem knows full well the answers:

> To taste the salt of the stars
> in the sea. To love another
> more than oneself. To know this
> is to know everything.
>
> Do you see how the dusk and rain
> are one?
>
> Do our bodies come to nothing?

In some ways, this is anti-workshop poetry, poetry with a billowing sweep that extends to a philosophical reach and seems to adhere strongly to a belief in both the power of poetry to access the unutterable, and its responsibility to convey deep feeling. In essence, this is Romantic Poetry, unfashionable perhaps in an age more forgiving of the charming lyric or the call to arms, but nonetheless striking for that.

> I spoke in code, replacing one sadness
> with another, as if sadness
> could stand in for the soul
>
> - 'A Soul Spreads Across the Sky'

VONA GROARKE

| SELECTORS' COMMENT

ANNE MICHAELS

Within a short span of time, I lost many of those closest to me, intimates of thirty years or more, among them the writers John Berger and Mark Strand, my longtime editor Ellen Seligman, my parents…

What words can we have for the last weeks and hours before the imminent death of one we love? A time both urgent and utterly suspended. What words for the overpowering loss of a shared inner life, of ideas, intention, a shared language – let alone the loss of every other intimacy?

It is a time of silence and muteness, and desire so extreme it is rendered chaste.

No words are restrained or spare enough, but *All We Saw* tries to render language chaste.

Music has a form for silence, but language must create a form (line breaks, syntax, white space…) to express not only silence, but the difference between silence and muteness.

These poems try to name the suspended moment – weeks and hours – before "desire forcibly / is renamed / grief / the precise space between / those two words".

To love as if we'd choose even the grief. Love does not die. We keep what belongs to us.

The poems in *All We Saw* are for John and for Mark. These poems were written to assert that "death must give / not only take from us."

ANNE RECOMMENDS

'Stilt Jack', in *John Thompson: Collected Poems and Translations* (Goose Lane Editions, 2015). 38 ghazals – one for each year of the poet's life – published posthumously. Mark Strand's *Collected Poems*. The restraint, of the later poems especially, amplifies their mystery. Mary Oliver's *Our World*. Not a book of poems, but Oliver honouring the memory of her partner, Molly Cook. A glimpse of how two people can live with each other and next to each other, for over 40 years.

I RECOMMENDATION

Do you see how the dusk and rain are one?

ASK ALOUD

To taste the salt of the stars
in the sea. To love another
more than oneself. To know this
is to know everything.

Do you see how the dusk and rain
are one?

Do our bodies come to nothing?

Not how we fall in love,
but how we fail in love.

Ask aloud what comes of us.

My love, do you understand me?
Not surmise. Sunrise.

Ask aloud what comes of us.

AHREN WARNER

Ahren Warner's first book, *Confer* (Bloodaxe Books, 2011), was a Poetry Book Society Recommendation and was shortlisted for both the Forward Prize for Best First Collection and the Michael Murphy Memorial Prize 2013. He was awarded an Eric Gregory Award in 2010 and an Arts Foundation Fellowship in 2012. His second collection, *Pretty* (Bloodaxe Books, 2013), was another PBS Recommendation. His third collection, *Hello. Your promise has been extracted*, brings together a new collection of poems with a sequence of the author's photographs. He is also Poetry Editor of *Poetry London* and currently lives in London.

HELLO, YOUR PROMISE HAS BEEN EXTRACTED

AHREN WARNER
POETRY BOOK SOCIETY RECOMMENDATION

BLOODAXE | £12.00 | PBS PRICE £9.00

Not since Ted Hughes wrote in response to Fay Godwin's photographs of the Calder Valley in *Remains of Elmet*, in 1979, has a sequence of poems been so successfully tied to an equally arresting sequence of photographs. In this case, the poet is also the photographer, and this seems to add a vital spark to the dynamism of the relationship. There are two languages of artistic expression always at work in this collection; the photographs have a way of casting the poems in the wash of their exquisite light. Set variously in Paris, Berlin and Budapest, Athens and Kiev, the tone of this collection is, in this era of shrinking boundaries of thought, compellingly European:

HELLO.

Your promise has been extracted like the cow-horned remains of molars long-soused in a Diet Coke marinade.

You may not have felt it but, whilst you loitered or stopped to ponder some frozen splinter of the Danube playing host to blue-lipped skaters slinking on a waning gibbous moon,

we pulled the bastard out.

Either side of this rich cluster of adjectives, and the prose-form of the line, are two photographs. On one page, the breaking down of a wall's render to reveal abstracted and anonymous shapes beneath; on the other, an oddly bleached soil in which a pavement-tree might grow, flattened out where the pavement has been repeatedly swept. In this way, time and again throughout this book, the two languages not only touch, but intersect, take on the responsibilities of one another, and sleep together in a gorgeous nightfall.

This is an extraordinary collection. Master of the single breath, and of the lengthening line, eschewing the occasional poem and as likely to address Celan as David Foster Wallace, Warner's poetics and experimental intelligence have moved a very long way in a very short period of time.

AHREN WARNER

The philosopher Kōjin Karatani has written that "if a stranger, an ostensible other, can be internalised, it is because he or she shares the common set of values. Strictly speaking, dialogue has to be with the one that engages the other who does not share the same set of rules". This thought returned again and again as I was putting *Hello. Your promise has been extracted* together: from my attempt to write in a way that acknowledges the pervasive nature of inflicted suffering – whether on the street or the screen – but that also respects the alterity of another's (or one's own) pain, to the very act of compiling a book that manoeuvres a collection of poems into confrontation with a sequence of photographic images.

A note on this curation of text and image: I have no interest in illustrative couplings of photograph and poem. Although it is true that, for example, there are photographs that I took in Kyiv and Athens, and poems that cite or are situated in both cities, the respective texts and images very rarely face each other. When they do, it is incidental. Rather, these poems are ordered in a way that I can only hope is effective, whilst the photographs are sequenced according to a separate logic of colour and tone.

What I am interested in is a certain silent event, a dialogue between – in this case – poem and photograph that sings in the aporia, the disconnect, between them. In this, as most of the time, I guess I'm thinking about Mallarmé's comment, in the preface to his *Un coup de dés*, that the blank space exists as both the "acceleration of rhythm, movement" and the "prismatic subdivision of the Idea", as well as Adorno's remark that "cognition that is to bear fruit will throw itself to the objects à fond perdu. The vertigo which this causes is an index veri; the shock of inconclusiveness, the negative as which it cannot help appearing… is true for untruth only".

AHREN RECOMMENDS

Nuar Alsadir, *Fourth Person Singular* (Pavilion); Ed Atkins, *A Primer for Cadavers* (Fitzcarraldo Editions); Yves Bonnefoy, *Poems* (Carcanet); Jacques Dupin, *Of Flies and Monkeys* (Bitter Oleander); David Harsent, *Salt* (Faber); Robert Herbert McCLean, *Pangs!* (Test Centre) Wayne Holloway-Smith, *Alarum* (Bloodaxe); Roddy Lumsden, *So Glad I'm Me* (Bloodaxe); Chloe Stopa-Hunt, *White Hills* (Clinic); Mark Waldron, *Meanwhile, Trees* (Bloodaxe); Catherine Wagner, *Nervous Device* (City Lights); C. K. Williams, *Falling Ill* (Bloodaxe).

Image credit Ahren Warner

WHEN IS TERROR NOT TERROR? When is terror
progress? Here, on Bessarabs'ka,

a beggar kneels, like beggars kneel
wherever. His head kisses a peel

of stone recovered from the snow;
he kneels on a sheet of filth that thaws

to a puddle of filth. Downriver, the river
freezes, Rodina-Mat rises, the Dneiper

is frozen mist, or the dry ice that capers
and flows around this salmon tartare,

this caviar, set here on a black, slate disc.
On Khreschatyk, you can buy anything:

just now a young, polite man asked me if
I'd like to buy a girl.

FLEUR ADCOCK

Fleur Adcock was born in New Zealand in 1934 but spent the years 1939-47 in England and has lived in London since 1963. Of her previous collections of poetry, all published by Bloodaxe Books, *Poems 1960-2000* was a PBS Special Commendation and *Glass Wings* (2013) a PBS Recommendation. She has also published translations from Romanian and medieval Latin poetry, edited several anthologies, including *The Faber Book of 20th Century Women's Poetry*, and written libretti and texts for a number of musical works. She was awarded an OBE in 1996 and the Queen's Gold Medal for Poetry in 2006.

HOARD

BLOODAXE | £9.95 | PBS PRICE £7.47

According to the Bloodaxe promo sheet, *Hoard* brings together for the first time poems which were too individual in tone and substance to fit the thematics of either *The Land Ballot* or *Glass Wings*, Adcock's previous two collections. The result is a finely wrought book which seems to have been inadvertently written while the other books were evolving, as if by some sort of ghostly pantograph.

Tackling subjects as diverse as her migration from New Zealand to England in 1963, the leader of the Jarrow March, Ellen Wilkinson, and her own return to visit North Island in 2015, there are fifty poems here, and they make a delightful sequence. Adcock is particularly good at exploring "...the charms of the special nib", the dying art of writing by hand, and the way in which "My private messages to myself / could remain in their workaday rags." She is even better at evoking the weighty awkwardness of the typewriter, now all but lost to us "...black and upright as a Model T Ford." In 'Six Typewriters' the old machines are monumentalised as far as the electronic typewriter which vanished almost literally overnight when word-processing brought about the writing revolution which changed everything for writers and of which Adcock chooses not to speak:

> the last one, a gift from my mother:
> electronic with adjustable spacing
> and a self-correct facility;
>
> so efficient that for years I spurned
> computers. Of them I shall say nothing.

Her particular strength is without doubt the crystalline lyric, fired by a gaze which is quietly but relentlessly penetrating. These poems carry in their stride what are often subtle devastations and there are tonal shifts, twists in diction, and shocks, not least her witnessing of an emergency caesarean during which "they snatched a skinned rabbit out of a hat".

THE SECOND WEDDING

Photographs were by courtesy
of the *Otago Daily Times*:

'Author Weds Poetess' – a shot
of the bride wearing a dazed smile

in her new husband's Land Rover.
Her bruises don't show up at all.

(How easy it is to get cheap
effects with not a word untrue.)

This was after the registrar
had waited for us to put out

our cigarettes, and married us.
It was his job, and we were there.

ANA BLANDIANA

Ana Blandiana was born in 1942 in Timişoara,
Romania. She has published 14 books of poetry, two
of short stories, nine books of essays and one novel.
Her work has been translated into 24 languages
published in 58 books of poetry and prose to date. In
Britain a number of her earlier poems were published
in *The Hour of Sand: Selected Poems 1969-1989* (Anvil
Press Poetry, 1989), with a later selection in versions
by Seamus Heaney in John Fairleigh's contemporary
Romanian anthology *When the Tunnels Meet* (Bloodaxe
Books, 1996). She was also President of the Romanian
PEN Club. In recognition of her contribution to
European culture and her valiant fight for human rights,
Blandiana was awarded the Légion d'Honneur (2009).

THE SUN OF HEREAFTER · EBB OF THE SENSES

TRANSLATED BY VIORICA PATEA & PAUL SCOTT DERRICK

BLOODAXE | £12.00 | PBS PRICE £9.00

The Romanian poet Ana Blandiana's third book in English translation appears in her seventy-fifth year and is the combination of two books, *The Sun of Hereafter* (2000) and *Ebb of the Senses* (2004). In many respects she is a poet of the old pre-1989 European dispensation, of the terrible Ceaușescu years when any writer worth anything was a voice of resistance and she bravely and conspicuously so. The language she forged then was one of metaphorical clarity. In this later compilation that clarity remains but its focus is, as the introduction to the books puts it, more "universal", dealing with social and spiritual questions. There are laments, despairs, consolations, meditations, the prospect of death never too far away. Always there is that clarity, a demanding precision of narrative and rhetorical form but little comfort. She talks of 'Old Angels':

> Old angels, stinking
> With a rank smell in their humid feathers,
> In their thinning hair,
> Their skin peeling off in patches of psoriasis,
> Maps of terrifying
> Unknown lands…

And in 'A Cathedral of Wool' of the sheer uncertainty

> No kingdoms of flora and fauna here,
> No stable states of matter,
> No line between the sea and sky,
> No shore between land and sea…

These are the late works, mostly short, of a beautiful, important poet, translated with clarity and measure by Paul Scott Derrick and Viorica Patea. It should take its rightful place in the European poetry section. But it is a good quarter for translations generally and the bilingual Welsh / English work of Menna Elfyn's *Bondo* with its various distinguished translators including the poet herself is worthy of celebration. The translations seem to be relatively free as to verse form, almost re-creations, but that is well within the compass of poetry translation. Peter Fallon's translations of Hesiod under the title *Deeds and Their Days* is also very welcome, a virtuosic comprehensive versing of the original into English. Marvellous.

GEORGE SZIRTES

SELECTORS' COMMENT

OCEAN

Salt on the skin, in sandals and hair,
And crust of salt on eyelash and lips,
Traces of a suffering unequal
Like the sea
That slides, disgusting, through jellyfish hovering;
The sad remains of beings
That seldom share in
The lonely despair
Of seconds slipping away
Or the bitter and
Salt-tinged taste on the tongue
Of half a century
Now consumed, of age, of the year, of motion.
Beach in August,
Ocean.

GUPPY PRIMER

Ruth McIlroy grew up in Kingston, Jamaica, was educated in Edinburgh, and now lives with her family in Yorkshire where she works as a freelance psychotherapist. Her poems have appeared in various magazines and anthologies. She has been commended or highly commended in the Kent & Sussex Poetry Competition, the Lancaster Literature Festival Competition, the Ver Poets Open Poetry Competition and the Templar Iota Shot Competition. In 2015 she was highly commended in the Philip Larkin East Riding Poetry Competition, and in 2017 she gained second place in the York Literature Festival Poetry Competition.

GUPPY PRIMER

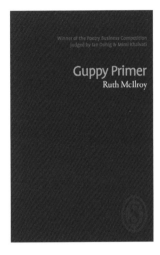

Winner of the Poetry Business Competition
Judged by Ian Oehig & Mimi Khalvati

Guppy Primer
Ruth McIlroy

SMITH | DOORSTOP | £5.00

Ruth McIlroy offers up a set of irresistible poems, full of warmth and humour. The title poem 'Guppy Primer' is one of the highlights of this collection. Here it's worth noting the precision of her image-making. McIlroy's instructions for fish breeding are exact: "Replace the water with aged good water, such as Bronx, NY / Tap water, which has a pH of 6.8." This is a poet who is strongly drawn to a world in which human sensibilities are interwoven with animal life.

Poems such as 'Spider Brain Tally' and 'Will you be my Bridesmaid' unleash an energy of wit into language itself. In 'Will you be my Bridesmaid', she reflects: "shall we call the bestest man 'waspish' / or 'of a certain age'".

Some of her work is powered by Scottish Gaelic to comic effect. McIlroy has an insatiable appetite for language. She is able to slip into varied voices as the poem demands. 'Just Idiot Talk' incorporates a Scottish Gaelic glossary. Here, McIlroy's definition of the title is "Just an idiolect consciously employed to gain acceptance from a dominant social group". For all its touches of humour, McIlroy's poetry is vibrant and memorable.

Gaps
    (to the tune of Streets of Laredo)

One night, at a lighthouse, I crept out to star-gaze;
I didn't remember the circling beam.
I sat on the bench and looked up at the heavens.
(Constellations – then nothing – constellations – the beam).

As I felt my way back by the curve of the sea-wall
It was,   , stars,   ,stars,   , stars,   ;
And to fill in the gaps then my brain took a fancy
(There was dream   not dream, beam not beam, dream   not dream, beam).

It pulled out some scraps of old song-lines and sayings
On the tip of my tongue; yes, like that, no, not that.
And I watched them come streaming, my dear higher functions,
Stuttering on in the dark; let them run, let them run.

I AM NOT HONEST

I am not honest.

My heart is a walnut;
I know nothing.

I enjoy dozens of exotic holidays a year.
I'm a girl but I've just always loved a scrap.

Anyway.

I do not suffer fools;
I suffer larks.
I suffer a peck of Dull Rubbish.

I am nothing
if not.

I believe myself to have become a little brutal.
£904 is paid every month into my bank account.

I do not know how to pronounce Eurydice.

RUTH MCILROY

ALARUM
WAYNE HOLLOWAY - SMITH

BLOODAXE | £9.95 | PBS PRICE £7.47

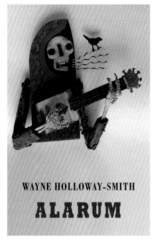

At the heart of this wonderful debut collection is a sequence, '(Some Violence)', which looks at working class masculinity, adolescent intimacy and awkwardness and the repositioning of the self that comes from being a working-class lad in a world of academia.

There's a real inventiveness and play in the language of *Alarum*, a surrealism as well but one that always feels as though it has a heart, a sense of being rooted in the truth. The fracturing of the self which happens in some of these poems, such as the wonderful 'Some Waynes', or the surrealising of the everyday means that the reader pays more attention to the ordinary occurrences that many of the poems deal with.

The body is central here, both in terms of the rarely written about but vital subject of male body image, and in terms of the violence enacted on the body and to the bodies of others. It is in these moments that a brilliant plainness comes through, such as here, in a quote from that previously mentioned central sequence:

> masculinity as   our neighbour's red and hairy knuckle
> masculinity as   my dad's head knocked back
> as a small man cursing

This seems to me to be a vital book about working class identity and how that shapes masculinity and the sense of self more generally. The final poem in the book, 'short', which recently won Holloway-Smith the Geoffrey Dearmer Prize ends with the lines:

> then nothing happens
> then nothing happens
> then it did

This is a collection which looks at small, fleeting moments of love, of despair, of aggression, and tilts them just enough to make us see them fresh, and see them for their true intricacy. Also, any book that throws in a casual reference to the great Geoff Hattersley is always going to win me over!

I GUEST SELECTOR'S 2017 CHOICE

47   ANDREW McMILLAN

ANDREW McMILLAN

Andrew McMillan was born in South Yorkshire in 1988; his debut collection *physical* was the first poetry collection to win The Guardian First Book Award. The collection also won the Fenton Aldeburgh First Collection Prize, a Somerset Maugham Award (2016), an Eric Gregory Award (2016) and a Northern Writers' award (2014). It was shortlisted for the Dylan Thomas Prize, the Costa Poetry Award, The Sunday Times Young Writer of the Year 2016, the Forward Prize for Best First Collection, the Roehampton Poetry Prize and the Polari First Book Prize. It was a PBS Recommendation for Autumn 2015. Most recently *physical* has been translated into Norwegian. He lives in Manchester.

GUEST SELECTOR

OTHER NEW BOOKS

THE MIGHTY STREAM: POEMS IN CELEBRATION OF MARTIN LUTHER KING
—— EDITED BY CAROLYN FORCHÉ & JACKIE KAY ——

Tying in with Newcastle's Freedom City 2017, this collection by Bloodaxe also serves to commemorate Dr Martin Luther King, Jr's visit to the city in 1967 when he was awarded an honorary degree at Newcastle University. Forché and Kay have arranged the works of over eighty poets into a comprehensive sequence remembering Dr King and regenerating the discourse and aims of the Civil Rights movement. This is an urgent and necessary collection, an eloquent surge embodying the "mighty stream" of the title.

BLOODAXE BOOKS | £12.00 | PBS PRICE £9.00

———————— SALT: DAVID HARSENT ————————

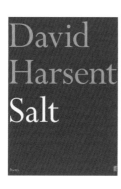

Harsent describes his collection of finely-crafted poems as "a series, not a sequence" with "broken chains of hint and harmony". This is certainly accurate, with semantic fields and common images resonating through over one hundred and seventy miniature works. Salt, blood, bone, plants, rooms, objects, glass, mirrors; reading the series becomes an investigation, assembling a tantalisingly elusive, possibly non-existent, narrative of memory and mortality.

FABER | HARDBACK £14.99 | PBS PRICE £11.25

———————— BANTAM: JACKIE KAY ————————

In her direct style, Kay examines her identity – familial, sexual, historical and national – in order to arrive at humanitarian conclusions of freedom and inclusivity. This is a collection which is both able to examine the past – for instance, the wars of the 20th Century – and confront contemporary crises. A significant element of this is the discourse surrounding refugees and their rights, which Kay unambiguously champions. This is not a poet who has time for subtleties in the face of oppression.

PICADOR | £9.99 | PBS PRICE £7.50

OTHER NEW BOOKS

SWIMMING POOL: ÁGNES LEHÓCZKY

Swimming Pool

Ágnes Lehóczky

An obsessive and expansive meditation on the art of swimming, Lehóczky is the perfect "aquatic flâneur" leading us with all the poise and equilibrium of the swimming body. Words pool into being as the reader swims through language to a fluid place "where your body ends (and) the pool begins". "Pool" becomes "the absolute trope" for truth and enlightenment, both a "universal whale" and a "cosmopolis". This is an utterly immersive experience.

SHEARSMAN | £12.95 | PBS PRICE £9.72

CERTAIN ROSES: ANGELA LIVINGSTONE

Livingstone frequently uses nature as a means to access the mysteries of being. Horticulture and the labelling of natural things makes the world more bizarre than if it was left unordered, this false sense of organisation dissonantly interacting with the secret impenetrable laws of the universe. And yet later the poet takes words like "earth" and "sky" and in them interprets some fundamental vocal link to what they signify. Counterpoints and uncertainty mark this mature, finely-crafted collection.

Angela Livingstone
Certain Roses
Poems 1980 - 2010

MICA PRESS | £8.50 | PBS PRICE £6.38

AND (POEMS 1970 - 2017): MICHAEL MACKMIN

Michael Mackmin

AND

Poems 1970 - 2017

This full collection of Michael Mackmin's poetry presents a beautiful yet tragic illustration of psychological turmoil and physical perception. Unexpected line breaks and fast-paced narratives create an intriguing impression, blurring the conventional distinctions between mind, body and external forces.

HAPPENSTANCE | £10.00 | PBS PRICE £7.50

| BOOK REVIEWS

OTHER NEW BOOKS

ON MAGNETISM: STEVEN MATTHEWS

Steven Matthews' latest poetry collection is an appreciation of both tranquillity and vitality, and associates the patterns of natural and human relationships with the concept of magnetism. Nostalgic for a Britain of the past, Matthews captures humanity on the edge: grasping for what is soon to be lost.

TWO RIVERS PRESS | £9.99 | PBS PRICE £7.50

THE MAGIC OF WHAT'S THERE: DAVID MORLEY

For David Morley, scientific observation has the potential to unearth magical patterns behind the real world. Stories of Morley's personal experiences and relationships are scattered among descriptions of rural life and animal biology, exposing the interplay between factual discovery and the power of imagination.

CARCANET | £9.99 | PBS PRICE £7.50

ONE FOR THE ROAD - AN ANTHOLOGY OF PUBS AND POETRY
EDITED BY STUART MACONIE AND HELEN MORT

One for the Road is a celebration of pubs, poetry and snippets of prose selected by Stuart Maconie and Helen Mort. Featuring over fifty poets, this pub crawl through poetry is the perfect companion for the next trip to your local, including anecdotes of last orders, glass-half-full poems and regulars reminiscing about now-closed drinking establishments or their favourite snug. A charming collection to delve into, whatever your poetic poison.

SMITH | DOORSTOP | £10.00 | PBS PRICE £7.50

OTHER NEW BOOKS

BINDWEED: MARK ROPER

BINDWEED
MARK ROPER

Roper begins by delicately progressing through subjects – birds, museum exhibits, zoology, botany, travel and foreign landscapes. This heightens the second half's dramatic turn, beginning with a violent fall from a cliff, moving in reverse to contextualise and explore the nature of this accident. The first half's themes are approached more warily after this event, and violence and mortality peer disconcertingly between images of birds and wildplants.

DEDALUS PRESS | £10.00 | PBS PRICE £7.50

AFTER RUSSIA THE FIRST NOTEBOOK: MARINA TSVETAEVA
TRANSLATED BY CHRISTOPHER WHYTE

The first of two notebooks of lyric poetry, *After Russia* (1928), represents the pinnacle of this great Russian poet's career. Both accomplished and experimental, these are poems of displacement and uncertainty, anguish and "soothing pain" which probe the limits of human expression and existence. And yet "light seeps through" with glimpses of "a happier world / than death".

SHEARSMAN | £9.95 | PBS PRICE £7.47

CROSSING THE MIRROR LINE: JUDITH WILLSON

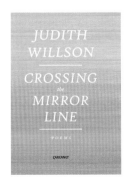

JUDITH
WILLSON

CROSSING
the
MIRROR
LINE

This debut collection by *New Poetries VI* contributor Judith Willson reflects, deflects and intersects time and place in a "double-going" dialogue. Whether inspired by nature, "the imprint of light" in photography or a painter who paints an empty drinking glass 5000 times, Willson cuts across the mirrored surface of the world. These are luminous, noctilucent and elusive works which find "tangles of light through stone" and arrive at quiet reflection: "Now this place is a mirror to itself".

CARCANET | £9.99 | PBS PRICE £7.50

BOOK REVIEWS

PAMPHLETS

Those hoping for a serving of Cope's trademark wit with a generous side of pathos will not be disappointed. This wonderful collection of Christmas themed poems will have readers laughing out loud and shedding a quiet tear. This reviewer cannot wait to sing the grammatically corrected version of Oh Come All Ye Faithful. Perfect self-gift or stocking filler material.

FABER | £7.99 |

CHRISTMAS CRACKERS: TEN POEMS TO SURPRISE AND DELIGHT
VARIOUS AUTHORS

With poems by the likes of Simon Armitage and Alison Brackenbury, this is a warm collection of Christmas themed poems suited to all moods. Poems like Wood's 'Bah...Humbug' for the anti-Christmas type to Duhig's 'White Rose Centre' for the typical happy-but-stressed-at Christmas type. There is no running theme between the poems but that's where the charm in the collection lies - you never really know what you're going to get.

CANDLESTICK PRESS | £4.95 |

BROKEN CITIES: KATY EVANS-BUSH

Katy Evans-Bush's wit is a biting one. Her poems are playful and well-observed, shining a comic and critical light onto modern life and human behaviour. Her work also has a sense of the historical, sweeping from allusions to creation and evolution in the fermenting milk-bottles, to the death of Wat Tyler, to a send-up of contemporary hipster culture in London.

SMITH | DOORSTOP | £5.00 |

PAMPHLETS

Adele Fraser presents an unapologetically furious single-poem pamphlet, serving both as a construction manual for the poet's selfhood and a defiant shout against a hypercritical external world. The poem aligns itself into neat stanzas and then rips itself apart, regenerating itself, mounting fresh assaults and retreating to its own battlements. *Intense World Fortress* is an emotional tour-de-force.

EYEWEAR   PUBLISHING | £6.00 |

——— CRYING FOR NO REASON: KIM KYUNG JU ———

In this pamphlet of translated poems Kim Kyung Ju, via translator Jake Levine, delivers fifteen works tightly interweaving space and the body, both becoming the other. Birds, water, hills, flesh, thighs, glaciers, urban furnishings and dense emotional weight are barely constrained beneath a flood of imagery shifting deftly between the mundane and the abstract, macro and micro, the external and the personal.

CLINIC | £5.99 |

——— PAISLEY: RAKHSHAN RIZWAN ———

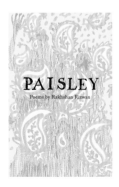

A striking debut collection which evokes the rich culture and history of Rizwan's native Lahore. Themes of belonging, migration and displacement abound, as Rizwan examines the split linguistic self of the migrant: "My voice is the mirror that breaks in Urdu". The patterns of her homeland are ever-present: "in a new country, let us dream of different paisleys". Combining free verse and complex ghazals, this is a powerful exploration of the role of women in Pakistan and beyond.

THE   EMMA   PRESS | £6.50 |

| PAMPHLET REVIEWS

PBS PRESENTS

PASCALE PETIT & JAMES SHEARD
Newcastle Centre for the Literary Arts

NCLA & The Poetry Book Society present a momentous evening with two of our finest recent Poetry Book Society Choice authors, Pascale Petit and James Sheard, reading from their PBS selected collections *Mama Amazonica* and *The Abandoned Settlements*. Tickets are available online from www.ncl.ac.uk/ncla.

30th November | 7.15pm | Culture Lab | £6

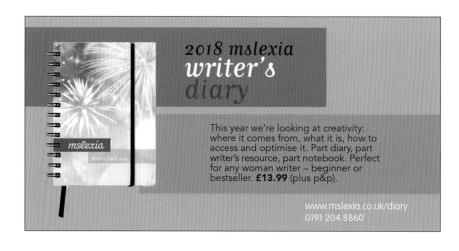

WINTER LISTINGS

NEW BOOKS

AUTHOR	TITLE	PUBLISHER	RRP
Fleur Adcock	Hoard	Bloodaxe Books	£9.95
Simon Armitage	The Death of King Arthur	Faber & Faber	£7.99
Neil Astley (ed.)	Land of Three Rivers: The Poetry of North-East England	Bloodaxe Books	£14.99
Justyna Bargielska, trans. Maria Jastrzebska	The Great Plan B	Smokestack Books	£7.99
Jo Bell & Jane Commane (eds.)	How to Be a Poet	Nine Arches Press	£14.99
Julia Bird	Now You Can Look	The Emma Press	£10.00
Robyn Bolam	Hyem	Bloodaxe Books	£9.95
Pat Boran	A Man Is Only As Good...	Dedalus Press	£10.00
Rachel Bower & Helen Mort (eds.)	Verse Matters	Valley Press	£10.99
Robert Burton	Lack Dream	Knives Forks and Spoons	£7.00
Helen Cadbury	Forever, Now	Valley Press	£8.99
Aleksandrs Čaks	Selected Poems	Shearsman Books	£9.95
Louise C Callaghan	Dreampaths Of A Runaway	Salmon Publishing	£10.00
Jenna Clake	Fortune Cookie	Eyewear Publishing	£10.99
Elaine Cosgrove	Transmissions	Dedalus Press	£10.00
Dick Davis	Love in Another Language: Collected Poems and Selected Translations	Carcanet Press	£20.00
Kwame Dawes	Prophets	Peepal Tree Press	£7.99
Paul Deaton	A Watchful Astronomy	Seren Books	£9.99
Marosa di Giorgio	I Remember Nightfall	Ugly Duckling Presse	£18.00
Tim Dooley	Weemoed	Eyewear Publishing	£10.99
Carol Ann Duffy	The Map and the Clock: A Laureate's Choice of the Poetry of Britain and Ireland	Faber & Faber	£20.00
Sasha Dugdale	Joy	Carcanet Press	£9.99
Margaret Eddershaw	Is That All There Is?	Mica Press	£8.50
Julie Egdell	Alice in Winterland	Smokestack Books	£7.95
T. S. Eliot	Collected Poems 1909–1962	Faber & Faber	£15.99
Alan Felsenthal	Lowly	Ugly Duckling Presse	£12.00
Julian Flanagan	Cooking with Cancer	Mica Press	£8.50
Carolyn Forché & Jackie Kay (eds.)	The Mighty Stream: Poems in Celebration of Martin Luther King	Bloodaxe Books	£12.00
Erin Fornoff	Hymn to the Reckless	Dedalus Press	£10.00
Naomi Foyle (ed.)	Blade of Grass: New Palestinian Poetry	Smokestack Books	£9.99
Graham Fulton	Equal Night	Salmon Publishing Ltd	£10.00
Robert Garnham	Zebra	Burning Eye Books	£9.99
Mark Granier	Ghostlight	Salmon Publishing Ltd	£10.00
Daniel Groves & Greg Williamson (eds.)	Jiggery-Pokery Semicentennial	Waywiser	£10.99
Caroline Hardaker	Bone Ovation	Valley Press	£6.99
David Harsent	Salt	Faber & Faber	£14.99
Jenn Hart & Clive Birnie (eds.)	Best Poetry Book in the World	Burning Eye Books	£12.99
Rachael Hegarty	Flight Paths Over Finglas	Salmon Publishing Ltd	£10.00
Wayne Holloway-Smith	Alarum	Bloodaxe Books	£9.95
Ishion Hutchinson	House of Lords and Commons	Faber & Faber	£12.99
Jackie Kay	Bantam	Picador	£9.99

WINTER LISTINGS

NEW BOOKS

AUTHOR	TITLE	PUBLISHER	RRP
Anja Konig & Liane Strauss (eds.) & illustrated by Emma Wright	Emma Press Book of Beasts	The Emma Press	£10.00
Ágnes Lehóczky	Swimming Pool	Shearsman Books	£12.95
S. J Litherland	Composition in White	Smokestack Books	£7.99
Angela Livingstone	Certain Roses	Mica Press	£8.50
Eamonn Lynskey	It's Time	Salmon Publishing	£10.00
Michael Mackmin	And (Poems 1970-2017)	HappenStance Press	£10.00
Stuart Maconie & Helen Mort (eds.)	One for the Road	smith|doorstop	£10.00
Lisa Matthews	Callisto	Red Squirrel Press	£8.99
Steven Matthews	On Magnetism	Two Rivers Press	£9.99
Joan McBreen	Map and Atlas	Salmon Publishing	£10.00
Iggy McGovern	The Eyes of Isaac Newton	Dedalus Press	£10.00
Anne Michaels	All We Saw	Bloomsbury Publishing	£16.99
Drew Milne	In Darkest Capital: Collected Poems	Carcanet Press	£20.00
David Morley	The Magic of What's There	Carcanet Press	£9.99
Conor O'Callaghan	Live Streaming	The Gallery Press	€11.95
Fani Papageorgiou	The Purloined Letter	Shearsman Books	£9.95
Yogesh Patel	Swimming with Whales	Skylark Publications	£9.99
Sylvia Plath	The Letters of Sylvia Plath: Volume I	Faber & Faber	£35.00
Sylvia Plath	Winter Trees	Faber & Faber	£10.99
Sylvia Plath	Crossing the Water	Faber & Faber	£10.99
John Powell Ward	Instead of Goodbye	Cinnamon Press	£8.99
Wendy Pratt	Gifts the Mole Gave Me	Valley Press	£9.99
Shivanee Ramlochan	Everyone Knows I Am a Haunting	Peepal Tree Press	£8.99
Lola Ridge	Collected Early Poems	Little Island Press	£16.99
Mark Roper	Bindweed	Dedalus Press	£10.00
Michael Rosen	Listening to a Pogrom on the Radio	Smokestack Books	£8.95
Alexandra Sashe	Convalescence Dance	Shearsman Books	£9.95
Aidan Semmens	Life Has Become More Cheerful	Shearsman Books	£9.95
Pnina Shinebourne	Pike in a Carp Pond	Smokestack Books	£7.95
Stevie Smith	Collected Poems and Drawings of Stevie Smith	Faber & Faber	£35.00
Ian Stuart	Quantum Theory for Cats	Valley Press	£6.99
Paul Sutherland	New and Selected Poems	Valley Press	£20.00
Paul Sutton & illustrated by Julia Scheele	The Diversification of Dave Turnip	Knives Forks and Spoons	£8.00
Anne Tannam	Tides Shifting Across My Sitting Room Floor	Salmon Publishing	£10.00
James Thornton	The Feynman Challenge	Barbican Press	£9.99
Simon Turner & illustrated by Mark Andrew Webber	Birmingham Jazz Incarnation	The Emma Press	£5.00
Robert Walton	Sax Burglar Blues	Seren	£9.99
Ahren Warner	Hello. Your promise has been extracted	Bloodaxe Books	£12.00
Carol Watts	When blue light falls	Shearsman Books	£9.95
David Wheatley	The President of Planet Earth	Carcanet Press	£12.99
Mike White	Addendum to a Miracle	Waywiser	£9.99
Jay Whittaker	Wristwatch	Cinnamon Press	£8.99
Judith Willson	Crossing the Mirror Line	Carcanet Press	£9.99
James Womack	On Trust: A Book of Lies	Carcanet Press	£9.99
Asha Lul Mohamud Yusuf	The Sea-Migrations	Bloodaxe Books	£12.00

BOOKS